If There Demons, Perhaps There Were Angels

William Peter Blatty's Own Story of The Exorcist

Illustrated by Rae Smith

SCREENPRESS BOOKS

First published in this form in 1999
by ScreenPress Books
8 Queen Street, Southwold, Suffolk IP18 6EQ

Originally published as the introduction to
William Peter Blatty on The Exorcist
From Novel to Film
Bantam Books 1974

extracted, edited and reprinted by permission of the author

Photoset and Printed in England.

A CIP Record for this book is available from the British Library.

ISBN 1901 680 34 7

For information on forthcoming film books from
ScreenPress Books please contact the publishers
at the address above or:

fax: 01502 725422
email: screenpressbooks@hotmail.com
website: www.screenpress.co.uk

If There Were Demons,
Then Perhaps There Were Angels

n 1949, while a junior at Georgetown University in Washington, DC, I read in the August 20 edition of the *Washington Post* the following account:

In what is perhaps one of the most remarkable experiences of its kind in recent religious history, a 14-year-old Mount Rainier boy has been freed by a Catholic priest of possession by the devil, it was reported yesterday.

Only after 20 to 30 performances of the ancient ritual of exorcism, here and in St Louis, was the devil finally cast out of the boy, it was said.

In all except the last of these, the boy broke into a violent tantrum of screaming, cursing and voicing of Latin phrases – a language he had never studied – whenever the priest reached those climactic points of the 27-page ritual in which he commanded the demon to depart from the boy.

In complete devotion to his task, the priest stayed with the boy over a period of two months, during which he witnessed such manifestations as the bed in which the boy was sleeping suddenly moving across the room.

A Washington Protestant minister has previously reported personally witnessing similar manifestations, including one in which the pallet on which the sleeping boy lay slid slowly across the floor until the boy's head bumped against a bed, awakening him.

In another instance reported by the Protestant minister, a heavy armchair in which the boy was sitting, with his knees drawn under his chin, tilted slowly to one side and fell over, throwing the boy on the floor.

The final rite of exorcism in which the devil was cast from the boy took place in May, it was reported, and since then he had had no manifestations.

The ritual of exorcism in its present form goes back 1,500 years and from there to Jesus Christ.

But before it was undertaken, all medical and psychiatric means of curing the boy – in whose presence such manifestations as fruit jumping up from the refrigerator top in his home and hurling itself against the wall also were reported – were exhausted.

The boy was taken to Georgetown University Hospital here, where his affliction was exhaustively studied, and to St Louis University. Both are Jesuit institutions.

Finally both Catholic hospitals reported they were unable to cure the boy through natural means.

Only then was a supernatural cure sought.

The ritual was undertaken by a Jesuit in his 50s.

The details of the exorcism of the boy were described to the *Washington Post* by a priest here (not the exorcist).

The ritual began in St Louis,continued here and finally ended in St Louis.

For two months the Jesuit stayed with the boy, accompanying him back and forth on the train, sleeping in the same house and sometimes in the same room with him. He witnessed many of the same manifestations reported by the Protestant minister this month to a closed meeting of the Society of Parapsychology laboratory at Duke University, who came here to study the case, and was quoted as saying it was 'the most impressive' poltergeist (noisy ghost) phenomenon that had come to his attention in his years of celebrated investigation in the field.

Even through the ritual of exorcism the boy was by no means cured readily.

The ritual itself takes about three-quarters of an hour to perform. During it, the boy would break into the fury of profanity and screaming and the astounding Latin phrases.

But finally, at the last performance of the ritual, the boy was quiet. And since then, it was said, all manifestations of the affliction – such as the strange moving of the bed across the room, and another in which the boy's family said a picture had suddenly jutted out from the wall in his presence – have ceased.

It was early this year that members of the boy's family went to their minister and reported strange goings-on in their Mount Rainier house since January 18.

The minister visited the boy's home and witnessed some of the manifestations.

But though they seemed to the naked eye unexplainable – such as the scratchings from the area of the wall in the boy's presence – there was always the suggestion, he said, that in some way the noises may have been made by the boy himself.

Retaining his skepticism in the matter, the minister then had the boy stay a night – February 17 – in his own home.

It was there, before his own eyes, he said, that the two manifestations that he felt were beyond all natural explanation took place.

In one of these the boy's pallet moved across the

floor while his hands were outside the cover and his body rigid.

In the other the heavy chair, with the boy immobile in it, tilted and fell over to the floor before the minister's amazed eyes, he said. The minister tried to overturn the chair while sitting in it himself and was unable to do so.

The case involved such reactions as neighbors of the boy's family sprinkling holy water around the family's house.

Some of the Mount Rainier neighbors' skepticism was startlingly resolved, it was reported, when they first laughed it off, invited the boy and his mother to spend a night in their own "unhaunted" homes, only to have some of the manifestations – such as the violent, apparently involuntary shakings of the boy's bed – happen before their eyes.

The article impressed me. And how coolly understated that is. I wasn't just impressed; I was excited. For here at last, in this city, in my time, was tangible evidence of transcendence. If there were demons, there were angels and probably a God and a life everlasting. And thus it occurred to me long afterwards, when I'd started my career as a writer, that this case of possession which had joyfully haunted my hopes in the years since 1940 was a worthwhile subject for a novel. In my youth I had thought about entering the priesthood; at Georgetown had considered becoming a Jesuit. The notion of course was unattainable and ludicrous in the extreme, since with respect to the subject of my worthiness, my nearest superiors are asps; and yet a novel of demonic possession, I believed – if only I could make it sufficiently convincing – might be token fulfilment of deflected vocation. Though let me make clear, if I may – lest someone rush to have me canonized – that I would never write a novel that I thought would not engross or excite or entertain; that I thought would have a readership of fifteen people. (It has often worked out that way, yes; but I didn't plan it.) If walking out of church you should pick up a Daniel Lord homiletic treatise from the vestibule pamphlet rack, you will not, I can virtually assure you, see 'as told to Bill Blatty' under Father Lord's name. But if one has a choice among viable subjects and one can do good along the way by picking *that* one . . . well, that is the little one can say of my motive.

As the years went by, I continued my studies in possession, but desultorily and with no specific aim. For example, I made a note about a character on a page of a book called *Satan*:[1] 'Detective – "Mental Clearance Sale".' The words, in quotes, would turn up eventually very deep in the story, as a thought of Kinderman, the homicide detective in the novel; but at the time I made the note, I knew nothing of its context. Finally, however – I think it was in 1963 – the notion of possession as the basic subject matter of a novel crystallized and firmed.

But the problem was that no one else liked the idea. Not my agent. Not Doubleday, my publisher at that time. Even my dentist thought the notion was rotten.[2] So I dropped the idea. I was a comedy writer; I had never written any-

1 Frank Sheed (New York: Sheed & Ward, 1952). I cannot recommend this book too highly for those interested in studying certain aspects of possession.
2 He endeavoured instead to seduce my interest, the cosmic rays being strong that day, towards fictionally exploiting 'the romance of dentistry'.

thing 'straight', except a few forged letters of excuse from my mother when I'd been absent from school the day before. ('Well, it hurt right here, Sister Joseph. Pardon? How could I have cancer for just one day?') I was doubtful I could do it; even more doubtful than Doubleday, perhaps, which would extend us from doubt into negative certitude.

But sometimes something, someone, helps. In December 1967, at a New Year's Eve dinner at the home of novelist Burton Wohl, I met Marc Jaffe, editorial director of Bantam Books. He asked me what I was working on. Finding the shortest line at the unemployment office, I told him; and then spoke of possession. He warmed to the subject matter instantly. I wondered if he was drunk. He suggested publication of the book by Bantam. I was then supporting the entire cast of Birnam Wood and requested an advance large enough to carry me for a year. He said, 'Send me an outline.'

What could I send him? The small scrap of paper with the cryptic notation about the detective? I had no plot. I had only the subject matter, some hazily formulated characters and a theme.

So I wrote him a long letter. I began by detailing what I knew of the incident of 1949, including some rather bizarre phenomena that had been bruited about on the Georgetown campus at the time: for example, a report that the exorcist and his assistants were forced to wear rubber windjammer suits, for the boy, in his fits, displayed a prodigious ability to urinate endlessly, accurately and over great distances, with the exorcists as his target.[3]

3 This report was false and later proved to have been a distortion of a similar and factual phenomenon whereby the boy could *spit* in such a manner, even with his eyes shut tight, or, as they sometimes were, physically shielded from his targets.

THE FACT OF GOD MADE VISIBLE

I went on to discuss the positon of the Church on the matter:

It cautions exorcists that many of the paranormal phenomena can be explained in natural terms. The speaking in 'unknown tongues' (unless it is part of intelligent dialogue), or possession of hidden knowledge, for example, can be explained in terms of telepathy – the possessed may simply be picking the knowledge out of the brain of the exorcist or someone else in the room. And as for levitation, Hindu mystics reputedly can manage it now and then, and what do we really know about magnetism and gravity? The 'natural' explanations are, of course, somewhat mystical themselves. But the occurrence of one or two of these phenomena, exorcists are cautioned, does not justify assuming one is dealing with true possession. What the Church does tell its exorcists is to go with the laws of chance and probablility, which tell us that it's far less fanciful to believe that an alien entity or spirit has control of the possessed than to believe that all or most of these paranormal phenomena are likely to occur all at once through purely natural causes. When all of them occur, and psychological causes are eliminated, then try the cure.

Still loftily avoiding such crass considerations as a discussion of plot, I nimbly leaped to the next sure peak – my intended theme:

Is there a man alive who at one time or another in his life has not thought, Look, God! I'd *like* to believe in you; and I'd really like to do the right thing. But twenty thousand sects and countless prophets have different ideas about what the right thing is. So if you *are* out there, why not end all the mystery and hocus-pocus and make an appearance on top of the Empire State Building. *Show me your face.*

We follow through by thinking that God doesn't take this simple recourse, this *reasonable* recourse, and therefore isn't there. He isn't dead and he isn't alive in Argentina. He simply never lived.

But I happen to believe – and this is part of the theme of the novel – that if God *were* to appear in thunder and lightning atop the Empire State Building, it would not affect (for long, at least) the religious beliefs of anyone who witnessed the phenomenon. Those who already believed would find the incident a reinforcement of their faith; those who did not already believe would be impressed for a while, but with the passage of time would convince themselves that what they saw was the result of either autosuggestion, mass hypnosis, or hysteria, or massive charlatanism involving nuclear energy and NASA. On a theological level, I happened to believe that if there is a God who is somehow involved with us and our activities he would *refrain* from appearing on top of the Empire State Building, because he would ultimately only cause trauma for those who *did not will* to believe, and thereby increase their guilt. The Red Sea's parting and the raising of Lazarus are not viable entries to religious belief. The trick to faith lies not in magic but in the *will of the individual.*

The novel would ask, I went on to explain, what effect a

confrontation with undisputed paranormal phenomena would have on the book's main characters: the atheist mother of the boy (as I then intended the victim should be; I had named him Jamie), and the priest of weak faith called in for the exorcism, whom I first named Father Thomas.[4] This thematic aspect would prove only a suggestion of what it would become in the book I eventually wrote, expressed by Father Merrin as follows:

> I think the demon's target is not the possessed; it is us . . . the observers . . . every person in this house. And I think – I think the point is to make us despair, to reject our own humanity, Damien: to see ourselves as ultimately bestial; as ultimately vile and putrescent; without dignity, ugly, unworthy. And there lies the heart of it, perhaps: in unworthiness. For I think belief in God is not a matter of reason at all; I think it finally is a matter of love; of accepting the possibility that God could love us . . .

And perhaps even this would seem merely an insight compared to the stronger, more encompassing theme that would spring from the Jesuit psychiatrist's act of ultimate self-sacrifice and love: the theme I call 'the mystery of goodness'. For in a mechanistic universe, where the atoms that make up a human being should logically be expected, even

4 Later on I renamed him John Henry Carver. I thought this aspect of the theme would work better if the priest were black and had come to the priesthood to escape from the slums and his boyhood identity; for then his resistance to the notion of possession in the face of levitating beds could be partly ascribed to his rejection of what he thinks are the superstitions related to his Haitian parents. The reason I abandoned this characterization was my fear of falling into the trap of writing Sidney Poitier.

in the aggregate, to pursue their selfish ends more blindly than the rivers rush out to the seas, how is it there is love in the sense that a God would love and that a man will give his life for another?[5]

Because it is true and embedded in reality, this theme would appear of itself in the inevitable developments of my plot, that plot which at the time of my letter to Jaffe was a beast as mythical as the unicorn. And so I 'vamped', as we mental swindlers often say. And then a murder, predicted long before by my subconscious[6] when I scribbled that note about a 'detective', indeed did appear to me. 'The killer is the boy;[7] the mother knows this, and against the eventual arrest of her son,' I wrote to Jaffe:

> The mother seeks psychiatric help to establish the boy was deranged at the time of the murder. The effort proves unpromising. She then seizes upon the device of calling in the psychologically intimidating forces of

5 It is useless to argue that unlike atoms, men have a higher intelligence, for this merely serves to help us rush all the more quickly.

6 I believe that my subconscious, once it has the necessary raw material (data and research) and sufficient prodding (sweat), does most of my plotting; and that it knew, by the time I had made that notation, almost the entire plot of *The Exorcist*, slipping portions to my conscious mind a little bit at a time. I remember, for example, being so surprised at the moment it occurred to me that Burke Dennings, and not an offstage character as originally planned, would be the demon's murder victim, that from my desk I cried out aloud, 'My God, Burke Dennings is going to be murdered!' Yet an early and seemingly accidental detail – Denning's habit of tearing off the edges of pages of books or scripts and then nervously twisting and fiddling with them – would later prove vital to a major piece of plotting. What we often call inspiration, I think, are in fact subconscious disclosures.

7 I wish to make it clear that in the 1949 case no killings or deaths of any kind were involved. Two priests were injured, however, one to the extent that for weeks he could use only one hand for the lifting of the chalice when saying mass.

the Catholic Church in an effort to prove (although she doesn't believe it for a moment) that her son is 'possessed' – that it was not Jamie but an alien entity inhabiting his body who commited the murder. She resorts to the Church and requests an exorcism; and soon it is arranged for a priest to examine the boy. She grasps at the desperate and bizarre hope that if the exorcist concludes that the boy is possessed and is able to restore him to a measure of normalcy, she will have a powerful psychological and emotional argument for securing both the release of the boy and the equally important release (even if the boy is imprisoned) from humiliation and degradation. The exorcist selected for the task is, by the one coincidence permitted us, the priest who has lost his faith.

Ultimately, the boy is exorcized. Although his fate at the hands of the law is not the concern of this novel. Our concern is the exorcist. Has his faith been restored by this incredible encounter? Yes. But not by the exorcism itself, for finally the exorcist is still not sure what really happened. What restores – no; *reaffirms* – his faith is simple human love, which is surely the fact of God made visible.

Virtually none of this plot survived; nor did my notion that 'the alien entity possessing the boy should be a woman who claims to have lived in some remote period of history, possibly Judaea in the time of Christ; and who attacks the exorcist psychologically by claiming an acquaintance with Christ, then proceeding to describe him in demythologozing, disillusioning terms'.

Jaffe shopped my letter at some hard-cover houses,

hoping to bring them in on the deal and thus share in producing the required advance. But a book about possession by a writer of comedy? Whose books, while they didn't sell fewer copies than *The Idylls of the King* in its Tibetan translation, certainly didn't sell any more? No one was interested, a phenomenon to which I'd grown accustomed, but which surely should have given Marc Jaffe second thoughts. But Jaffe held fast, and Bantam, on its own, at last came up with the advance. Only then did I begin to believe that perhaps I could write the book.

After some intervening screenplay assignments, I undertook a period of intensive research early in 1969. From the outset I was biased by training and religion in favour of belief in genuine possession. Furthermore, replace the word 'demon' with the words 'disembodied malevolent intelligence', and one has a concept not repugnant to reason or in apparent contradiction to the laws of matter, whatever they happen to be this year. Aldous Huxley's *Devils of Loudun* makes a devastating argument to the effect that the seventeenth-century epidemic of demonic possession in a convent of Ursuline nuns in France was a fraudulent, hysterical manifestation; yet even Huxley observes:

> I can see nothing intrinsically absurd or self-contradictory in the notion that there may be non-human spirits, good, bad and indifferent. Nothing compels us to believe that the only intelligences in the universe are those connected with the bodies of human beings and the lower animals. If the evidence for clairvoyance, telepathy and prevision is accepted (and it is becoming increasingly difficult to reject it), then we must allow that there are mental processes which are largely inde-

I THINK I'VE LOST MY FAITH
I SHOULD'VE BEEN THERE I WASN'T THERE

pendent of space, time and matter. And if this is so, there seems to be no reason for denying *a priori* that there may be non-human intelligences, either comple-tely discarnate or else associated with cosmic energy in some way of which we are still ignorant.[8]

Teilhard de Chardin, the Jesuit philosopher-palaeontolo-gist, once proposed that what we think of as matter and spirit are but differing aspects of something else, some third and fundamental reality in which matter and spirit com-mune. And indeed, the views of modern physicists on the ultimate nature of matter seemed to be leaning towards support of Chardin, seemed increasingly to be edging towards something like mysticism, a paradoxical conse-quence of the steadily deeper probings into the Chinese box of the atom. Consider the neutrino. It can speed through a planetary thickness in a twinkling, yet has no mass and no magnetic or electrical charge. Real, yet lacking fundamental properties of matter, the neutrino is a ghost.[9]

All well and good. Possession is possible, I thought. But where were the documented cases? Where was even *one* well-documented case? 1949. I thought of that. The story in the *Washington Post* seemed factual; and yet, finally, how could I tell? Only an eyewitness could corroborate it for me. In an earlier try at tracing the exorcist, I had queried the *Washington Post*, but couldn't find the reporter who

8 *The Devils of Loudun* (New York: Harper & Row, 1952).
9 Physics now tells us that on the subatomic level matter as we know it does not exist; that on the subatomic level there are no 'things', only processes; and that the clockwork universe of the mechanists has been destroyed. We have the additionally mystical notion, which won for its discoverer the Nobel Prize, that a positron 'is an electron *moving backwards in time*'.

had written the story; and the names of the exorcist and the fourteen-year-old boy who was the victim had never been known. I'd also queried the Jesuits I'd known while at Georgetown who were still on the campus. None could help.

So I searched the literature of possession. To begin with, though in time they reached back to ancient Egypt, the published sources, notably those in which the insights of psychiatry were fully reflected, were not only few in number, but also repetitious. And of the cases cited, over 90 per cent were conceivably attributable to fraud, delusion, a combination of both, or misinterpretations of the symptoms of psychosis, particularly paranoid schizophrenia, or of certain neuroses, especially hysteria and neurasthenia. Eighty per cent of the victims were women, moreover, a ratio so disproportionate as to suggest, as opposed to possession, a common disorder once alluded to as *furor uterinus*, an expression that speaks, I would think, for itself. This would surely account for the extraordinary lewdness of speech and behaviour that I found to be present, without exception, in every case of so-called demonic possession. And it surely is significant that Tourette's Syndrome, a still mysterious neurological disorder only recently isolated and labelled, is primarily characterized by the sudden, apparently unmotivated and unpredictable onset of a usually irresistible compulsion to shriek out a torrent of verbal obscenities not noticeably lacking in nauseating grossness.

A few of my findings were intriguing: the reporting of a common symptomology in cases widely separated with respect to both time and place; and cases where the victims were very young children. Both tend to make hysteria, fraud or delusion more remote as explanations of possession.

16

How would an eight-year-old boy, for example, come to know its classic symptoms? It is possible. But likely?

And consider what happened to four of the exorcists sent to deal with the outbreak at Loudun. Three of them, Tranquille, Lactance and Lucas, successively appeared to be possessed themselves, and while in that state died, perhaps from cardiac exhaustion. The oldest of these men was forty-three. The fourth, Surin, a noted intellectual and mystic, a truly good man, only thirty-three, became totally insane and so remained for twenty-five years. If these exorcists were faking, they carried it far; if temporarily hysterical, they were so in defiance of a psychiatric principle that tells us that hysterics do not blossom overnight; and if hysterical beforehand, though of differing backgrounds, then their hysteria must surely have been the determining criterion employed by the cardinal who picked them for the mission, for how could we otherwise account for the coincidence involved in his selecting four closet hysterics? I do not find these possibilities alluring to reason. And it was certainly known well before the events at Loudun that symptoms suggesting possession could in fact be caused by mental illness: 'The too credulous,' the Church warned would-be exorcists in the Acts of the Synod of Rheims, 'are often deceived, and . . . lunatics often declare themselves to be possessed and tormented by the devil; and these people nevertheless, are far more in need of a doctor than of an exorcist.' That statement was made in 1583.

Moreover, what was I to think of cases of possession in which the subject's personality, voice and mannerisms altered so radically that people around them actually believed they were dealing with someone else? It is useless to resort to 'dual personality' as an explanation. The competent psychiatrists[10] who authored *The Three Faces of Eve* make the candid admission that while Eve's disorder disappeared in apparent response to treatment based upon a certain diagnosis of the problem, that diagnosis depended on the interaction within equations of concepts like 'mind', 'personality' and 'hysteria'; but in fact the reality back of these labels is still unknown. In physics, when working certain equations, one assumes that light is composed of particles; but in working other equations, the assumption is that light is composed of waves. It probably is neither.[11] But it cannot be both. And that either type of equation 'works' does not prove either assumption concerning light; it proves only that the equation works. So in attempting to explain possession, one might as well say 'demon' as 'dual personality'. The concepts are equally occult.

Before Eve Black's case, the great psychiatrist Morton Prince had treated a case of dual personality in which one of the newcomers, hardy 'Sally', who knew everything her other personalities were doing whereas they knew nothing of her activities, claimed to be a 'spirit' and refused to be therapeutically murdered, so that Prince at last resorted to 'exorcism'. By taking her on her own terms he was able to argue her into returning whence she had come. In a like vein, following publication of *The Exorcist* I was to hear from a noted psychologist that he believed that some of his former patients had been 'obsessed', the second stage of possession in which the attack is from the exterior. This

10 Corbett H. Thigpen and Hervey M. Cleckley (New York: McGraw-Hill, 1957).
11 Or, like the neutrino, evidence that matter is finally spirit?

psychologist, Dr Alan Cohen, a Ph.D. from Harvard who practises in San Francisco and coauthored *Understanding Drug Use*,[12] told me that in paranoid schizophrenic subjects experiencing auditory hallucinations, the verbal patterns of association of ideas should be identical to the patterns in the content of what is hallucinated, since both patterns have a common source. But in certain of his patients, Cohen told me, these patterns were totally dissimilar, thereby suggesting separate intelligences. Cohen alluded to the two little boys, aged ten and eleven, who killed by crucifixion a three-year-old boy in San Francisco, each explaining independently that 'a voice' had told him to do it; he told me further that the former chief psychologist at Mendocino State Mental Hospital in northern California, Dr Wilson Van Deusen, believed that many patients in the disturbed ward in that institution were possessed;[13] and that he went so far as to practise therapeutic exorcism on occasion.

All interesting, indeed. Any yet all these findings taken together did not constitute the slimmest reed of evidence. The case for demonic possession had finally to rest on what was plentifully lacking at Loudun: the reliably

12 *Understanding Drug Use: An Adult's Guide to Drugs and the Young*, Alan Cohen and Peter Marin (New York: Harper and Row, 1971).
13 As reported in *Newsweek* (11 February, 1974, p. 61), other psychiatrists agree: '. . . there are some psychiatrists who no longer dismiss exorcism as a crude, pre-Freudian method of handling emotional disturbance. Milwaukee psychiatrist Alan Reed Jr says he will not rule out possession as an explanation for some forms of extreme psychic disorder. "In the whole field of spiritualism, mysticism, religion and the human spirit," says Reed, "there are things so minimally understood that almost anything's possible." "I believe all that stuff," admits Dr Walter Brown, a psychiatrist at Mount Sinai Hospital in New York City. "In a way, all psychoanalysis and psychotherapy are forms of exorcism, of getting rid of demons."'

witnessed and reported occurrence of so-called paranormal phenomena. Levitating mattresses are very 'out front'.

Of course I found many such cases reported in the literature. And at times the eyewitness observer – the noted ethnologist Junod, for example – surely had to be counted as reliable. So too must William James, the great psychologist, who investigated the case of a girl in Watseka, Illinois, who underwent a total and abrupt transformation of personality and identity, claiming for months to be someone named Mary Roff, who turned out to be a real person whom she had never met: a sixteen-year-old girl who had died in a state insane asylum years before. James declared the 'spiritist explanation' of the case 'the most plausible' one available. And Carl Jung, it is perhaps little known, was connected with another case of possession for almost a year.[14] The case involved a fifteen-year-old girl, the daughter of friends. Normally dull-witted, she manifested three distinct personalities, one of them a chatty and eloquent old man who spoke High German, a dialect completely unknown to the girl. She demonstrated telepathic abilities and an astoundingly accelerated intelligence, all of which phenomena were frequently witnessed first hand by Jung, who found in them no possibility of fraud.

But the case involving James lacked paranormal phenomena, and the case involving Jung, while it apparently did exhibit such phenomena, was, however, totally lacking in the fits of rage, the malevolent activity and the demonic

14 Fully described in his 'On the Psychology and Pathology of So-Called Occult Phenomena', *Psychiatric Studies*, in the *Collected Works of C. Jung*, Bollingen Series XX (Princeton, NJ: Princeton University Press, 1957).

self-identification that characterize so-called demonic possession. And of all the other cases of demonic possession I studied, almost all exhibiting paranormal phenomena had occurred no later than 1900, with some dating back several centuries. I constantly found myself asking: Who were the witnesses? Who had written the report I was reading? Could I trust his veracity and judgement? Did he witness the phenomena himself? If so, how much time intervened between events and the preparation of the report? Or was the record based on hearsay? And if so, how far removed was it from the eyewitness source?

In an ordinary circumstance when there is continuing and universal testimony that such-and-such a thing has occurred, we allow for inaccuracies and falsehood but accept the main core. There are extant a number of differing Deluge stories. There are those who cannot accept the Old Testament account of a massive ark that bore animals two by two in its hold. And who can take literally the Gilgamesh epic? The point is that we do accept the *core* of these stories: that at some point in history mankind experienced a devastating flood.

Yet I could not apply that kind of thinking to possession. Not that such reasoning is invalid, for in life – and sometimes in science, especially physics – very little is 'proved' before we give it assent; instead, what we do is make prudent judgements. But prudent judgements do not satisfy when dealing with the supernatural, for the ultimate issue is too important; the issue is God and our hope of resurrection. Thus, on hearing a second-hand report from Martha and Mary to the effect that the tomb is empty, that 'He is risen,' I would first stroll over to the tomb and examine it myself; and then, if the women claimed to have personally witnessed the actual resurrection,[15] I would have a little chat with them to try to determine if they had been 'stoned' at the time. I would also pull their files from Roman Intelligence to check out their character, their integrity and their record of 'prowler' calls to the police. Only then would I begin to formulate a prudent judgement based on what they had said.

And so with possession. I felt that if I couldn't write the novel with conviction I probably wouldn't want to write it at all; for how could it possibly turn out well? A hollow heart cannot excite.

I found a case that was relatively recent: 1928. In Earling, Iowa. There was only one account of the event, a printed pamphlet written by a monk. The pamphlet carried photographs of the principals. Paranormal phenomena were cited. One in particular gave me pause. It was stated that the victim, a forty-year-old woman, would repeatedly and forcefully fly up from her bed as if hurled like a dart, head first, at a point above the bedroom door, where she would hang suspended by her forehead, as if tightly glued to the spot. An extraordinary image! I instinctively felt that it could not have been invented. Moreover, while phenomena tended to repeat themselves in the cases I had studied, this was one I had never before heard the likes of. And yet my overall reaction to the pamphlet was a shrug. Perhaps some who are familiar with the pamphlet were impressed, by which I do not imply that my threshold of credulity is higher than theirs, as should be evident to anyone who examines my record of box-top mail-ins at the Post Toasties plant, notably the one in response to an offer of a Dick Tracey

15 Merely a 'for instance'. According to Gospel accounts, they did not.

'two-way radio ring'. But the tone of the pamphlet seemed so overly credulous, so replete with pietistic asides and exclamations, that it turned me off. I reacted illogically, I suppose, as the basic phemomena might still have been factual; but the pamphlet made me think of 'Crazy Mary', a friend of my mother's who during my boyhood visited seven churches a day and saw Our Lady of Fatima in the alphabet soup. I simply didn't trust it. And the people involved were unfortunately dead. That ended Earling, at least for me.

Next I called upon numerous Jesuit friends in the hope that they might lead me to someone now living who had actually performed an exorcism: maybe someone from the foreign missions, for in Asia and Africa possession is common. But I had no luck. I came closest with Father Thomas Bermingham, who had taught me at Brooklyn Prep and was master of studies at St Andrew's-on-Hudson, a Jesuit seminary, at the time I sought him out. He recalled that in his earliest years in the priesthood a Jesuit quartered at the seminary was known to have performed an exorcism. Withdrawn and never known to speak, he haunted the wooded walks alone, a blank, burned-out look in his stare. He was late into his thirties. His hair was shock-white. It had happened in the exorcism, I was told.

The story caused my pilot light to flicker back on; and in the back of a book that I used in my research, I have recently discovered a small notation that it doubtless inspired: 'Exorcist white-haired man called out of retirement to do it again. He dies early and assistant takes over.' But Father Bermingham couldn't remember the original model's name.

So I tried something utterly illogical: instead of asking more Jesuits who'd been in the neighbourhood when the incident had taken place, I called a Jesuit friend of mine in

Los Angeles, thousands of miles away from the event. He gave me the exorcist's name and address.

I wrote to him. He answered with the following letter, from which I have deleted certain information for reasons that will be apparent:

Your letter, addressed to me at the — Retreat House at —, was forwarded to me here, where I have been stationed for the past year. We have a mutual friend in Father —, SJ.

As you stated in your letter, it is very difficult to find any authentic literature on cases of possession; at least, I could not find any when I was involved in such a case. Accordingly, we (a priest with me) kept a minute account each day of the happenings each preceding day and night, one reason being that our diary would be most helpful to anyone placed in a similar position as an exorcist in any future case.

My hesitancy in giving you the details of the case of possession is due to two facts. First, —, who delegated me as the exorcist, instructed me not to publicize the case. I have been faithful to his instructions. Secondly, it would be most embarrassing, and possibly painfully disturbing, to the young man should he be connected in any way with a book detailing events that took place in his life some years ago. Since a case of possession is a very rare occurrence, he would certainly connect his own experience with any such account.

Some Jesuits living with me at — at the time were conversant with some of the events in the case; and, as often happens, as a story passes on, events are not correctly reported.

My own thoughts were that much good might have come if the case had been reported, and people had come to realize that the presence and the activity of the devil are something very real. And possibly never more real than at the present time. But I submitted my judgement to the instructions which I received from —.

I can assure you of one thing: the case in which I was involved was the real thing. I had no doubt about it then and I have no doubts about it now.

Should I be of any assistance to you within the limitations I have set forth in this letter, I would be glad to accommodate you.

I wish you every success in the important apostolate of the pen. You can do so much good with that gift.

The letter was electrifying, for at last I felt I was in touch with reality, with a good and sensible man. I wrote again and asked permission to see his diary, not for the purpose of reproducing any of its details in the novel I would write, but because I am Thomas and needed to put my own fingers in the wounds. But again the exorcist declined, citing the need to protect the boy; he would only assure me that the case had indeed involved unambiguous paranormal phenomena.

I later would learn that even a priest who had requested the material from the Washington archdiocese was told in 1952 that 'His Eminence [the Cardinal] has instructed me to inform you that he does not wish the case of exorcism of the boy in Mount Rainier discussed publicly. The parents of the boy made a very strong request to that effect and we have tried to shield them and the boy from any embarrassing publicity.' After *The Exorcist* was published, a number of periodicals and newspapers resurrected the original account of the case given out by the victim's minister; I had changed the boy in my story to a girl, although more to ease the exorcist's anxiety than from fear of doing any real harm to the boy, inasmuch as the specific locations, the characters and the story in my novel were not taken from the actual case, there being, as I have said and now repeat, no murders or deaths of any kind in the latter; and in addition, I utilized no paranormal phenomena peculiar to only *this* case of possession. Nevertheless, all this being said, it is a fact that the diary maintained by the exorcist was submitted, for their guidance, to two other people who were in contact with the boy and were to keep a watchful eye on the course of his recovery, and to the archives of two archdioceses; and that it came somehow to be in the files[16] of a city hospital where the boy for a time was confined and where some of the exorcism was performed. And it is also a fact that I have read it; that I have long known the name of the boy and where he lives; and can attest that the diary kept by the exorcist is in part, and beyond any doubt, the thoroughly meticulous, reliable – even cautiously understated – eyewitness report of paranormal phenomena.

The story in the *Post* proved accurate, except where it implied that the boy knew Latin. It is true that he was able to parrot long phrases, and even sentences, in Latin just spoken by the exorcist as part of the ritual; and that he always burst into fury at the exorcist's command of *'principio tibi . . .'*, the beginning of the first of the stern adjurations of the Catholic ritual of exorcism. But the parroting is

16 *Not* via the exorcist, who continued to exhort me never to reveal the boy's identity.

easily attributable to the heightened unconscious intellectual performance – sometimes fifty times normal – that is cited by Jung as a possible concomitant of certain forms of hysteria. And the rages were doubtless cued by the abruptly loud and commanding tone recommended for delivering the adjurations in the Catholic 'Instructions to Exorcists'. The 'unknown language' specification used by the Church as a sign of possession requires that the person allegedly possessed be able to engage in *intelligent dialogue* in that language. I cannot vouch for what may have happened prior to the exorcist's appearance on the scene; but certainly no intelligent dialogue in Latin was ever in evidence thereafter, even though the exorcist frequently demanded it of the alien intelligence controlling the boy's response in Latin to certain questions required by the ritual ('What is your name? When will you depart?'; and although the 'demon' (whatever ultimate reality may lie behind that name) protested at one point, 'I speak the language of the persons,' a seemingly childish, if not fraudulent, evasion.[17] But there was nothing evasive about the levitation of a hospital nightstand beside the boy's bed, which was witnessed by a physics professor from Washington University; nor could one so characterize a repeated and striking phenomenon not mentioned in the *Post* account: the various markings – described in the diary as 'brandings' – that appeared spontaneously

17 Although an identical claim in two earlier cases of possession was further explained by the possessing entities as relating to the absence, in the bodies of their hosts, of the muscular formations in the physical speech apparatus that develop with the use of a language; thus their efforts to speak another language not known to the host would be halting, if not laughable. In the cases cited, however, the languages were French and German; whereas Latin has never posed any such problem for high-school freshmen, with the possible exception of myself.

and without apparent cause on various parts of the victim's skin. Many times they were words clearly etched in fiery red block letters that were usually a little over two inches tall; other times they were symbols; at still others, pictorial representations. One of the words that appeared was SPITE. One symbol was an arrow that pointed directly at the victim's penis. And a very clear picture was that of a hideous satanic visage. But by far the most frequent and alarming of the brandings were lengthy lines that at times broke the skin, as if the boy had been raked with the prongs of an invisible miniature pitchfork. Or, one could say, claws.[18]

18 In both the novel and the film the levitation of the bedstand would translate into the levitation of the bed itself. Other phenomena taken from the actual case would be the rappings; lesser manifestations of telekinesis, such as the drawer popping out and objects flying around the room; the 'brandings' (the words on the victim's flesh, as just described); the transformation of the voice; new abilities (such as perfect pitch) never before manifested by the subject; paranormal strength; the bellowings; and a few lesser and more ambiguous phenomena, such as the accurate 'blindfolded' spitting. The transformation of Regan's face, the furring and lengthening of the tongue, did not come from the actual case, but were taken from countless other cases, and in fact are no less marked than occurs in certain types of hysterical disorders. The icy cold, the shaking of the room and the cracked ceiling did not occur in *any* of the cases I studied. Neither, of course, did the turning of the head, at least to the extent depicted in the film. As this scene was first shot, Regan's head turned *360* degrees! When I pointed out to Billy Friedkin that in such an eventuality the head would likely fall off and that 'supernatural' was not synonymous with 'impossible', the head turn was modified in the editing room. I still believed it to be excessive and unreal, but audiences loved it. Moreover, there is *some* factual basis for it. In the state of possession, and among hysterics, you will find one medical case after another in which the subject – no acrobat – was none the less able to perform such incredible physical contortions as bending over backwards and touching his heels with his head. What distinguishes possession – and pseudo-possession – from hysteria in this context is that the possessed subject, when performing these actions, seems to be doing so involuntarily, for throughout he shrieks in pain.

During brandings, the boy wore only his undershorts. No bedcovers hid his movements. His hands were at all times in view of the exorcist and his assistants and others in the room. One branding that ran from the boy's inner thigh to the top of his ankle, drawing blood, occurred while the exorcist was seated on the end of the bed, his eyes on the boy, and no more than about a foot away. Other of the brandings were on the boy's back. And one, the word SPITE, did not fade from his skin for over four hours.

The physics professor from Washington, having seen the hospital bedstand levitate rapidly upwards from the floor to the ceiling, later remarked that 'there is much we have yet to discover concerning the nature of electromagnet-ism', an observation impervious to challenge. But when we are confronted with the paranormal, is it valid, in this age of scientific awareness, to resort at the last to 'unknown forces'? We do not know all of the positive efficiencies of natural forces; however, we do know some *negative* limita-tions. In the words of the Jesuit Joseph Tonquedec, 'By combining oxygen and hydrogen you will *never* get chlor-ine; by sowing wheat you will never get roses . . . If any-one, sowing wheat, should believe that "perhaps" he might get roses, he must be in an abnormal state of mind.'[19]

I wrote the novel. It was finished by the summer of 1970.[20] As soon as I had made several Xerox copies (for I

19 *Les Maladies nerveuses ou mentales et les manifestations diaboli-ques*, p. 230; see also *Satan* (cited in note 1).
20 Had it not been for a friend, William Bloom, it might not have been finished until the following year; for on an evening in June, when I allowed him to read what I had written thus far – which was up to the point of Merrin's death – my plan was for Karras to continue the exorcism for one or two more months. Bloom said the reader would kill

never make carbons, which must mean I have a death wish), I took one to my neighbour, Shirley MacLaine. I had always felt inadequate and insecure in my handling of female characterizations, a bulletin certain not to stun like oxen any of the women in my life. And so when starting the novel, I had looked about for a model for Chris MacNeil, one who lived in a milieu that I knew very well and who also had a mental set and personality that would make the story work: a flipness of manner (masking vulnerability) and an earthiness of tongue that would help to keep the situation rooted in reality; whose 'I'm from Missouri" attitude would serve initially as the reader's point of view. This device would later provide what Anthony Burgess has called the 'nice irony' of *The Exorcist*: an atheist heroine who comes to believe that her daughter is possessed, in opposition to a Jesuit hero who does not. Though Shirley leaned more to agnostic at the time, she'd have been perfect as the model for Chris. And now I was bringing her the novel because I hadn't seen her in a very long time and because I'd had a little bit[21] too much wine and hoped to give her a happy surprise with Chris MacNeil. I lasted twenty minutes. I think my line about 'saving her career' must have done it, though it could have been my effort to show her some card tricks that I told her I had learned from Roy Rogers's horse. She steered me gently to my car after giving me a bag full of rocky road candy, which has always had an instantly sobering effect upon me, a reflex triggered by my need to be alert to defend the rocky road from aggressors, namely any-

---

me if I did that; the action was crying out to be at an end. This conversation convinced me to have Karras perform the actual exorcism in less than a minute of time.

21 Staggering quantities.

one at all who might ask me to share it. The candy was decidedly better than the dog food I'd once spied on a daintily wrapped dish in her refrigerator just before she conned me into taking several bites of it, calling it 'White Fang Pâté Parisien'; but I felt a bit glum at her fluffing off the novel as something she would read when she had 'a little time'. Four days later, though, she called me to tell me she had read it. She seemed touched by the characterization of Chris. There were even lines of dialogue scattered through the novel that she recognized as having said many years ago. How did I come to remember them? she asked me.

She asked me to drop by. I did; and at her home she spoke more about my memory. And then said that she would like to do the book as a film. Of course when I had brought her the book I had imagined that it might be a film; and certainly Shirley would play Chris MacNeil. But I had no idea how such a film could be made; and now Shirley, who had entered into a partnership for the making of feature films with Sir Lew Grade, the English producer, was talking of cancelling the first of the films in which she was set to star and going with *The Exorcist* in November.

It was all too sudden. I had laboured nine months, often fourteen hours a day, every day, at a novel that had to be convincing to work. To achieve this texture of reality, I had resorted to techniques such as setting up a situation (Chris's party) where the reader would assume that Chris and Karras would finally meet, that seemed designed in fact just in *order* that they meet, and then after this buildup *not* having them meet; to having Chris called 'Mrs MacNeil' by some characters and 'Miss MacNeil' by others; and even to writing in varying styles, each matched to the major character being dealt with.[22] So now I was tired and, as I said, unsure that a script could be done at all, at least by me. There were so many problems involved in adapting the novel to the screen. First, the internalizing by Karras. And how could the paranormal happenings be shown? How could Regan's demonic transformations be managed? How could the complex events of the novel be accomplished in a film less than eight hours long? Finally, how could I write such a script by September in order to shoot it in November?

I thought it was impossible. And immediately agreed to do it.

But the wearier part of me set conditions. First, we had to make a satisfactory deal; and, second, I wanted to produce the film. Have you any idea why I insisted on the latter, or what can happen to a screenplay when it leaves the writer's hands? Film is an industry[23] in which writers are either broken or wind up senselessly murdering strangers in the streets. For example, Ivan Tors, the creator of the *Flipper* series, had, in addition to the dolphin, a monkey and a pelican in subordinate roles in his 'pilot' (establishing) script. The head of NBC television called Tors to his office and assured

22 Merrin, complex and poetic and filled with concrete images of nature. Chris, simple, and direct and ordinary as a supermarket shopping cart. Karras, elegiac and haunted by images resonating pain in the minor particular. The styles blended with the appearance of Kinderman.
23 I use the word advisedly and in a sense that could be sobering to some. For a film is made with stockholders' money. Its purpose is profit. When an artist isn't using someone else's money, he is free to create his art for art's sake. But when his creation is financed by a studio, which borrows the money from a bank, the loan must be repaid; otherwise the value of the stock goes down and some pensioner may lose her life's savings. Simple decency therefore dictates that the artist not make a silent film in which the actors all meditate for seventeen hours.

him that the project was 'fantastic'. In fact, it was going on the air that Autumn with a guaranteed run of thirty-nine weeks. Tors was elated but – 'There's just one little change that I'd like you to make,' the head of the network went on to tell him. 'Get rid of the dolphin and build up the part of the pelican.' And when *The Wizard of Oz* was first screened for studio heads, MGM's Louis B. Mayer recommended that the Kansas sequence, in which 'Over the Rainbow' is sung, be cut from the picture because it was 'boring', an act which was followed by Paramount's head of production, Marty Rackin. At the cocktail party celebrating the showing of the 'rough cut' of *Breakfast at Tiffany's*, Rackin remarked to Blake Edwards, the film's director, 'Well, I can tell you one thing, Blake: the song has got to go.' The song in question being 'Moon River'. ('Are you running with me, Jesus?')

Fortunately, none of this advice was followed. But too often the producer or the director or the actor or his wife will commit more obscenities of change upon a script than Launce's dog wrought against the gentlewoman's farthingale in *Two Gentleman of Verona*. Oh, there are times when it can work in reverse: when direction and editing and performance can transform a weak script into something wonderful and essentially other than it was. But more often, and especially in the area of comedy, substantial tampering with the script inevitably leads to its destruction. I once wrote a caper script, for example, in which the first two acts built to an effort by talented rogues to rob 'the unrobbable bank of the West', a bank constructed by bank robbers specifically for storing their stolen loot, since in no other bank would it be secure. For two whole acts we are shown the bank's impregnable defences. We come to like the rogues, and hope they will succeed, since if they don't they will die. For two whole acts we watch them make elaborate preparations, while being kept in the dark about the specifics of their plan. How will they do it, the audience wonders. And that was what the film was supposed to be about. But the director,[24] known in the business as a genius with comedy, suggested 'just one little change' in the script: namely, that the leader of the rogues do a 'High Hopes' type of song with a bunch of kids complete with choreography. Never mind that it paralysed the momentum of the plot and utterly destroyed the pace; far worse, it put us on *overtime*. And the film would run long. To solve this problem, the director suggested[25] that we cut out the entire robbery sequence. The robbery! 'We just see them coming up on the bank and then dissolve to them loading the gold on the cart,' he explained. The advice wasn't followed, thanks to Malcolm Stuart, the producer. But the role that was written to be played by Rex Harrison ended up being played by Zero Mostel, and the role intended for Melina Mercouri was played instead by the ever-iridescent Kim Novak.

I was determined that this wasn't going to happen with the script of *The Exorcist*. Thus my insistence on producing it. But we never came to terms. In spite of Shirley's great enthusiasm, Lew Grade's offer for rights to the film was very low. In my straitened circumstances I probably would have accepted it except that in that case the producer would not be me but Robert Fryer, then most recently the

---

24 Whom I do not name, for he has suffered enough, his crime having served as his punishment as well.
25 On three separate occasions in my presence, which eliminates the possibility that he wasn't really serious.

producer of *Myra Breckenridge*. Shirley was upset that I'd rejected this offer and instead took the lead in a rival work, *The Possession of Joel Delaney*. That decision ended, if for no other reason,[26] any chance of her playing Chris MacNeil. Chris still haunts her, however.[27] Since *The Exorcist* was published, she had several times told me of her conviction that the very blurred photo representing Regan MacNeil that appears on the jacket of the book is in fact a photograph of her daughter which I'd 'lifted' surreptitiously from her house. 'Have you ever seen "baba au rhum in a blender" written in lipstick on your bathroom mirror?' I asked her the last time she made the accusation. I explained that whenever I burglarize movie stars' homes to steal photographs of their children, I write those words in lipstick on a mirror. 'It's my mark,' I told Shirley. In reality the jacket art and photo were created by Harper & Row. When first I saw the photo, in fact, I thought that it strongly resembled *my* daughter.

Around the time the Lew Grade negotiation ended, Bantam put the novel out to bid for publication by a hard-cover house. Of the four good firms to whom it was submitted, two became active, if not vigorous, bidders, with Harper & Row at last bravely doubling the previous last bid that had been made by Random House. A third house receiving a submission, Knopf, had Thomas Tryon's *The Other* upcoming on its schedule; and a four-person editorial staff at McCall Publishing (now defunct) unanimously rejected the

26 Billy Friedkin preferred Ellen Burstyn for the role of Chris. Ellen got the part and proved to be magnificent.
27 As the novel in a way haunts Sachi, her daughter; for various columnists, hearing that Shirley was the model for Chris, have published irresponsible innuendoes that Sachi was 'possessed' at the time, and that the novel is her story, an absurdity cruelly put to use by Sachi's schoolmates. I repeat, there is not a shred of truth in the report.

novel altogether, which may prove some consolation to frustrated writers.

I went to New York and heard Harper's suggestions for revisions of my first draft. I was asked to drop the prologue, which I considered but didn't do; and to make the ending less obvious, which I did. In my original version of the epilogue, both Chris and the reader realized fully what Karras has done: that he has lured the demon out of Regan's body into his, and after doing so is aware that the demon, when in total control of his body, will murder Regan and anyone else in the household and then leave him, once more in control of his body, to face the horror he has wrought. Karras, apprehending this, makes a superhuman effort to regain full control of his body and battles the demon's will just long enough to hurl himself out the window in a final, saving act of love. But the ending, as I'd written it, flirted with bathos, and perhaps even married it. You may judge for yourself. Here is the relevant section of the original epilogue:

> Chris went upstairs to Regan's bedroom. She looked in from the doorway and saw her standing at the window, staring out. Her hands were clasped lightly behind her back. Chris paused. She felt a twinge of worry. Slowly she moved forward to the window. There she stopped. She examined the child's face. Regan was slightly frowning as at sudden remembrance of forgotten concern. She looked up at her mother. 'What happened to the man?'
>
> 'The man?'
>
> Regan nodded. 'The one who jumped out of the window. Ya know? The man in the funny black dress.'

Wide-eyed, Chris sagged to one knee. She took hold of her daughter's hands and held them firmly. 'You saw a man jump?'

Regan nodded solemnly. 'Is he all right?'

Chris held her breath. 'Honey, tell me.' She paused, controlling her voice. 'Can you remember – can you remember what happened?'

'Well, he jumped.'

'Honey, why? Do you know?'

Regan frowned.

'Do you remember why he jumped?'

'Well, it's kind of . . . well, funny.' Regan looked off. 'I mean, I think I might have dreamed it.' Regan shrugged. 'Well, it sort of was crazy.'

'Just tell me, honey! Tell me whatever you remember!'

'Well, the man . . . well, he was saying . . . I mean, talking to some animal or something . . .'

'An animal?'

'Well, something . . .' Regan bit her lip, her brow furrowed. 'He was telling it to go, like – to get out. You know? And then he said . . .' She paused, as if groping for the memory, 'He said – if it came out it could go inside *him*. And then – well, it seemed like it *did* go inside him. This animal or something. It went in him.' She looked at her mother. 'I think that part I *must've* been dreaming. Don't you think?'

Chris stared numbly. 'Honey, tell me what else!'

'Well, this man started acting real crazy an' stuff. Like he was fighting with someone.'

'Fighting?'

'Uh-huh. But there was nobody there, though. Just

him. An' he was saying . . .' She squinted at the form-ing recollection. She turned to her mother. 'I remem-ber. He was saying that he wouldn't let it hurt you.'

'Let it hurt me?'

'Well, hit you, sort of. And me. I mean, all of us. He said he wasn't going to let it hurt us. And that's when he jumped.' Regan pointed to the window. 'I mean he ripped off the covering, first. *Then* he jumped.' Regan frowned. 'Mother, why are you crying?'

'Because I'm happy that you're well again, baby. I'm just crying 'cause I'm – happy – that you're well.'

'Is the man all right, Mom?'

Chris looked down. 'Yes, honey. The man is all right. He's resting.'

'In the hospital?'

Chris nodded.

'Can we go and see him, Mom?'

Chris lifted her face. The tears ran freely. 'Yes, honey,' she smiled. She clasped Regan's hands. 'Some-day . . .'

And so I rewrote it. The basic elements remained the same but I made the exposition more oblique.[28]

While still in New York and in the midst of revising the manuscript, I received a call from a William Tennant, repre-senting Paul Monash, who had just produced *Butch Cassidy and the Sundance Kid*. Would I enter an exclusive negotia-tion with his client for an option on the book? Tennant asked. I would. For Monash offered to meet my terms. We

---

28 In view of widespread misunderstandings of both the novel and the film, I now wonder if I made the correct decision. And certainly do miss the implication of Chris accepting faith, indicated in her 'Someday . . .'

made a deal whereby Monash would have six months to get a major studio to make the film. If he failed, all rights to the property reverted to me and I would keep the money he had advanced. If he succeeded, I would write the script and produce, with Monash acting as executive producer. And he did succeed. He made a deal with Warner's to make the film.

But soon we had some disagreements. Paul, a bright man and a writer himself, was in favour of changing the local of the action from Washington, DC, as it was in the novel; didn't like the 'colourful' treatment of Kinderman; thought that Chris shouldn't be an actress, said we shouldn't use the prologue of the novel, which introduces Merrin in Iraq;[29] and wanted to eliminate Merrin entirely. None of this pleased me. Then came further disagreements involving the studio. I don't remember what I did then; I must have blacked out. But according to a rumour abroad in some circles, I pilfered some documents (Shirley MacLaine just sat up and paid attention) relating to my deal that showed a lack of . . . well, shall we just call it due regard for fair business practice?[30] According to the rumour, which of course is preposterous, I picked a day to go to Warner's when I knew that Paul Monash would be at Universal. And it being the lunch hour, and Monash's temporary secretary busy chatting in an office opposite, it is said that I entered the reception area of Monash's office; and that the secretary

---

29 As an archaeologist working on a dig at the ruins of Nineveh, for Merrin was modelled on Pierre Teilhard de Chardin, even his self-confessed frailties, which are taken from letters that Chardin wrote to his friend Madame Zonta; his love of matter; and his view of the relationship existing between matter and spirit, which he thought to be merely differing aspects of some third, more fundamental reality.
30 More commonly known as 'screwing the author'.

then returned to ask me who I was; and that I told her, 'William Faulkner', requested some coffee, the urn being visible in Monash's office, and then inquired if I might use the phone; and while using the phone – now being seated behind the reception desk and in view of the secretary, who'd gone back across the hall – I rummaged through drawers for a key, found it, went into Paul's office for another cup of coffee, lunged at a file drawer labelled 'A to E', unlocked it, found some documents filed under 'Exorcist' that I thought of unusual interest, tucked them in a copy of *Fortune* magazine, went out the office and two doors down to the Warner Bros. Xeroxing room, made copies of the documents, tucked them back inside the copy of *Fortune*, returned the originals to the file, locked it, sat down again at the desk, picked up the phone and dialled 'time and temperature' while returning the key to where I'd found it; and then disappeared into the Burbank fog with a clutch of documents which seemed to prove conclusively that crimes against the author had indeed been committed and which because they were in my possession, impelled the studio to buy Monash out and make me sole producer of the film.

I began the script. I compressed the first third of the book into only thirty-three pages. And then I further decided to eliminate the subplot relating to Elvira, the servant Karl's daughter. I hated to do that. The Elvira subplot not only added a dimension to Karl, but was intended to illustrate Merrin's belief that out of evil there finally always comes good; for Kinderman's relentless investigation of Dennings's murder results in Elvira, a heroin addict, at last being hospitalized and on the road to cure. But there simply wasn't time and the subplot had to go. So too did the novel's subtle hints that the killer and desecrator might be Karras. Thought I did insinuate it, at first, in the sequence that begins in the Jesuit refectory at Georgetown and ends with Karras and a young Jesuit on a platform at the top of the steps from which Dennings was probably[31] pushed to his death. Karras says he always tries to make it to the platform around that time to watch the sunset. The Georgetown University clock booms the hour: 7.00 p.m. Dennings plunged to his death at 7.05. And Karras, who once blacked out at a time when a desecration was taking place, is surely a candidate for somnambulism produced by an 'unconscious rebellion' against the Church; for not only is he filled with compulsions of guilt but he was refused in his request for a transfer to New York so that he might be close to his mother, who since that time has died alone.

Again, though, there wasn't time and most readers of the novel had failed to pick up on the suggestion anyway. And so finally I cut the scenes. Even so, I wound up with a first-draft script that ran to over two hundred pages. If shot, it would result in a four-hour film. But I decided, like Scarlett O'Hara, that I would 'worry about that tomorrow'.

It was June and by now the novel had been published. I could tell by the mail I was getting. Some of it was nice. Some was not. And some of it, letters from a number of readers seeking help because they thought themselves to be possessed, was very pathetic.[32]

I heard from Jack Douglas, the humourist, who began his

31 The likely assumption at that point in the story.
32 Although one from a woman who complained she had an incubus (demon lover) seemed not only rational but touched with humour. She'd taken her complaint to a psychiatrist who told her 'most women would give their right arm' to have her problem.

letter with the comment, 'I sure wish Karras was still alive – I've got a couple of kids I'd like to have him take a look at.' Another who wished that Karras had lived was my friend the exorcist. For in a letter which remarked on the authenticity of the book, he decried the impression that Karras had 'lost'. I was stunned. For he thought it was the *demon* who impelled Karras out through the window to his death. It was a view shared by many other readers, I learned, and accounted in part for my hate mail. With such an interpretation, my novel was received by the reader as a definite 'downer' and construed by many to mean that evil finally triumphs. I really don't know what to do about 'speed readers'.[33] Shooting them certainly comes to mind. Although most of the hate letters that I received – and by far the most virulent – had nothing to do with sloppy reading, but came instead from those who presumed to lecture me obscenely about obscenity. Useless explaining to them that obscenity lies not in words but in every contravention of the Sermon on the Mount; useless citing favourable reviews in a number of religious periodicals, among them the *Civiltà Cattolica*, the Vatican literary journal.[34] One woman to whom I had pointed out the latter, in fact, wrote again to me, screeching, 'If the Pope likes your book that *proves* it's rotten.' And that helped. Until then the attacks had hurt a

33 One reviewer thought the action took place in Boston. Another complained that I knew nothing about construction, citing my introduction of a character in the prologue (Merrin) who one 'never sees again'. And the *Saturday Review* somehow got the notion that Karras was Jewish.
34 Religious press reactions to the film have been widespread and equally favourable. Among them is a review in the *Catholic News*, the official newspaper of the archdiocese of New York, which stated that '*The Exorcist* is a deeply spiritual film'; and the arch-conservative *Triumph* magazine, which published a rave review.

bit. But at that point I realized that they had come, in the main, from people who hated themselves.

Not so with some others, perhaps mainly those who felt the book's shocking aspects were unnecessary. I did not share their belief. To begin with, the descriptions of demonic behaviour are authentic (as are also the descriptions of rites at Black Mass; and everything else in the book that relates to satanism or possession). Furthermore, and purely apart from dramatic considerations – the need for something so unthinkably horrible (the crucifix masturbation scene) that it drives an atheist to a priest – if you're attempting to present possession as possible evidence of an unutterably evil and malevolent intelligence, then you must back it up both in concrete detail and in the viscera. You cannot say, 'Regan then did something awful'; for if demons exist, that is not the way to argue it; and not the way to make us abhor what is evil. Oddly – and significantly, I think – the only blast at the novel, in print or in the mail, from any formal religious source, emanated from a Jesuit named Raymond Schroth, who assailed me in *Commonweal*, basing his attack not on 'obscenity' but on his feeling that *The Exorcist* fostered belief in Satan, thus prompting a return to 'the superstitions of the Middle Ages'. He suggested I ought to be writing about social action. Perhaps he was right.[35]

I myself, in considering the question of Satan's existence,

35 Though not about everything; for in the article in *Commonweal*, he asserted that 'Père de Tonquedec, the old Parisian Jesuit, one of the most renowned exorcists of recent times, reportedly told his fellow Jesuits that he had never encountered an authentic case of diabolic possession.' But another Jesuit who read Schroth's article wrote to me stating, 'In 1961 I stayed for a few days at the Jesuit residence on the Rue de Grenelle in Paris. After dinner I was sitting next to Father de Tonquedec in the

reflect upon the fact that every primitive culture has had a myth about an evil being or 'magician' who comes to earth and spoils the work of the Creator; who introduces hatred, disease and death. Then I think of the soldier who deliberately throws himself atop a freshly hurled enemy grenade in order to shield his comrades from the blast. Not his children; not his sweetheart; not his mother: fellow soldiers. And I cannot help feeling, when I consider these things, that the world holds far more monstrous evil than can be accounted for solely by man, who is essentially good. I have not reasoned to this. I *feel* it.

But is Satan a single personal intelligence? Or Legion, a horde of evil entities? Or even, as has been conjectured, the stuff of the universe: matter itself, Lucifer working out his salvation through the process of physical evolution that ends in Teilhard de Chardin's 'omega point'. I surely do not know, not can I even make a prudent judgement. Whatever my beliefs concerning Satan's existence, however, we have no record of reliable data that would link him to possession. I know that will surprise many readers and reviewers. But historically, the 'demons' involved in possession and pseudo-possession rarely identify themselves only as Satan. And surely the chief of the fallen angels has far worse things that he could be doing. Even in terms of my novel, I have never known the demon's identity. I strongly doubt

---

recreation room. In the course of the conversation, I asked whether he had ever been involved in a real case of possession. I kept a diary during my trip with no thought that what I recorded would ever be of any significance. I just checked it and I find this entry under date of October 23 1961: "Father de Tonquedec told me that he certainly had encountered one real case of diabolical possession, and possibly two others."'

that he[36] is Satan; and he is certainly none of the spirits of the dead whose identity he sometimes assumes. If I had to guess, I would say he is Pazuzu, the Assyrian demon of the south-west wind. But I'm really not sure.[37] I know only that he's real and powerful and evil and apparently one of many – and aligned with whatever is opposed to love.

Now I put away the mail. It was time to select the film's director. My contract with Warner's called for a form of mutual approval whereby, before the signing of my contract, we were to shape a list of directors agreeable to both. The list we had agreed upon finally included Arthur Penn, Stanley Kubrick and Mike Nichols.

I had also suggested Billy Friedkin. I had met him years before. I'd been working with Blake Edwards on the script of a Peter Gunn feature called *Gunn.* Billy was up for the job of directing it; in first position in fact. Billy had never directed a full-length feature film. But all he had to do to change that fact was to read the script and then tell us he liked it.

He read the script and met with Blake and me for lunch at the Paramount commissary. Straight-on and very articulate, he was only twenty-six and with his horn-rimmed glasses looked like *Fiddler on the Roof*'s Tevye as a boy. But he wasn't about to ask God for any favours and proceeded to tangle with Blake on a sequence in the script that he thought should be cut, a sequence I had written. It was a very small point and he might have let it slide. But he didn't.

36 Perhaps the one instance of dreaded male chauvinism not bound to irritate women's liberationists.
37 The novel is ultimately what Billy Friedkin calls a 'realistic look at inexplicable events'. And only in fantasy can the author be omniscient. We can get inside the heads of humans; not of demons.

And blew the assignment of course. But I never forgot him. My previous experience with most directors had been that they would tell you your script was sensational, their only reason for taking low money, because frankly, they would confide, they needed a hit; and then when they'd been hired and were safely under contract, they would give your script to the FBI chief, instructing him, 'This should never see the light of day.' Friedkin, in that context, was a wonder.

Years later, I saw his *The Night They Raided Minsky's*. I thought it had movement and grace and sensitivity. It wasn't commercially successful but I liked it very much. I had a pet script in my trunk at that time. It was based on the novel I had written before *The Exorcist*, *Twinkle, Twinkle, 'Killer' Kane* (a.k.a. *The Ninth Configuration*), my first exploration of the mystery-of-goodness theme, although, despite the lurid jacket copy on the Curtis paperback edition, it had nothing at all to do with the occult.[38] It was set in a military rehabilitation centre and centred on a war of nerves between the psychiatrist in command of the centre and a number of inmates led by an astronaut who refuses to go to the moon on the grounds that it might be bad for his skin. Just prior to being committed, he is observed, while dining in the officer's mess, as he picks up a plastic

38 Let book people never cast stones at Hollywood. Compare the quotes that were used on the *first* Curtis edition of *Twinkle, Twinkle, 'Killer' Kane* – 'Nobody can write funnier lines than Blatty' (Martin Levin, *New York Times*) and 'Wild . . . with the verbal virtuosity of S. J. Perelman' (Richard Armour, *Los Angeles Times*) – with their jacket copy and front matter on the edition published following *The Exorcist*: 'The nerve-twitching chiller from the author of *The Exorcist*' and 'INVITATION TO EVIL! A grotesque old mansion that once used to belong to a silent horror movie star, and now was home to shrieking terror . . .'

ketchup squeeze bottle, squeezes a thin red line across his throat and then staggers over to a table where the head of the Space Administration is dining, falls across it in front of him and gurgles, 'Don't – order – the swordfish.' Another of the inmates, to round it out for you, is adapting the plays of Shakespeare for performance by a cast of dogs and 'cannot abide a Dalmatian that lisps'. ('Shrieking terror'!) It was what you might call bizarre material. I had hoped to direct it myself. But after seeing *Minsky's* I thought that the script would be safe with Friedkin. I sent it along to him. He liked it. But we couldn't find a studio that liked it. We'd put it away. Now, with *The Exorcist* film in preparation, his name leaped to mind and I submitted it to Warner's for inclusion in the list. They turned it down. But then one by one the directors on the list were pencilled out. Some had commitments that would keep them unavailable for almost a year. Arthur Penn was teaching at Yale. Stanley Kubrick could produce for himself, thank you kindly. And Nichols said he didn't want to hazard a film whose success might depend upon a child's performance.

Then there were none. So I suggested Friedkin again. Again they said no. And they asked if instead I'd be willing to consider another director whom I personally liked and who was talented and sensitive but whose work I none the less loathed. He'd been critically acclaimed for a film that consisted in the main of interminable reaction shots in which the characters stared at each other piercingly, thinking presumably staggering thoughts. Let us say that the name of that film was *Hypnosis* and the name of the director, Edmund de Vere. If he were to wind up directing *The Exorcist*, with a script of over two hundred pages, its running time couldn't be under three weeks. However, I agreed

– to be fair[39] – to screen a rough cut (generally, the first edited version, but minus music and finished sound, and in some cases optical effects) of de Vere's most recent work, which, I was assured, would 'change my mind'; it was 'absolute dynamite', 'so sensitive', I was told.

I screened it alone at the studio while a studio executive sat awaiting my reaction. And yes, it was sensitive. But so were Leopold and Loeb. And I felt that I was watching another murder, the victim in this case being pace. Entire novenas could be said during pauses in the dialogue.[40] This was all very well at Cannes, I supposed, but would surely be deadly for *The Exorcist.* Thinking the locale of the novel was Boston was but one indication of how readers often flew through the pages of the novel to gulp down further developments of plot. Slow pacing on screen would result in frustration and diminishing tension.

Midway through the screening I thanked the projectionist and left. I returned to the executive's office. On seeing me back an hour early he did a little leap about an inch off his chair, and I imagined his hair standing straight up on end just like Little Orphan Annie about to say, 'Yike!' when the news isn't really all that smashing.

He asked that I return to the screening room. The ending, he insisted, 'was the picture'. And how could I judge after seeing only half of it? There was also the need to forestall 'bad word of mouth', which would start with the projectionist's report to his friends that 'Blatty walked out on it half-

39 I lie. It was to give the *appearance* of being fair.
40 Directors who come up from the ranks of cameramen sometimes subordinate other considerations in a scene to what will make the best-composed 'picture'. De Vere had been an actor (and though never a star, was truly outstanding), and thus no doubt tended to indulge his casts.

way through, and he isn't even *bright'*; and which is how the public comes not to queue around the block on opening night for a film that hasn't been reviewed yet.

The executive had his secretary call the projectionist. She told him I'd had a headache but was feeling much better now and would be back to see the rest of the film. I returned to the screening room. And liked the second half of the film only very little more than I had liked the first. I didn't return to the executive's office. Depressed, I had dinner and then went to a movie. I went for diversion, not to study. But the film was Friedkin's *The French Connection*. And I went quietly berserk. The pace! The excitement! The look of documentary realism! These were what *The Exorcist* desperately needed.

I called the head of the studio. And soon the executives at Warner Bros. were screening *The French Connection.*

Billy Friedkin was hired.

WILLIAM PETER BLATTY
SIGNED COPIES OFFER

THE NINTH CONFIGURATION
a.k.a. TWINKLE. TWINKLE, KILLER KANE

ISBN 1 901 680 207

Paperback, illustrated throughout with stills from the film
£9.99

Some years after the release of *THE EXORCIST* William Peter Blatty tried again to persuade William Friedkin to film *TWINKLE, TWINKLE, KILLER KANE*.

Eventually Blatty decided to direct the film himself from his own adaptation of the novel. The film, entitled THE NINTH CONFIGURATION, is set in a remote castle in the Pacific Northwest which is being used by the US Government as a military asylum. Stacy Keach leads a fine ensemble cast playing a Marine Corps psychiatrist with a crisis of faith who encourages his patients to enact their fantasies as part of their therapy. He quickly proves himself to be more deeply disturbed than at first appears and finally sacrifices himself, Karras-like, to save one of his patients.

The film was released in several different versions and is hailed as a cult classic forming part of a loose 'trilogy of faith' with the film *LEGION* (*EXORCIST III*).

Recognised as an offbeat film which is both visionary and challenging, the dialogue throughout is extremely powerful and thought provoking, hilarious at times and endlessly quotable.

ScreenPress Books is pleased to announce that this previously unpublished screenplay will be available for the first time to coincide with the release on video of THE EXORCIST.

A limited number of copies of the book will be signed by William Peter Blatty, to reserve your copy please contact:

The Book Service
01206 255777

All signed copies will be reserved on a 'first come, first served' basis and your order will be held until the books are supplied.

Your credit or debit card will not be charged until the books are dispatched.

The price of £9.99 includes free post and packing.

Other screenplays and film books from *ScreenPress Books*.
All available with free post and packaging from *TBS Ltd*,
01206 255777

Contemporary British Cinema

THE FULL MONTY
Simon Beaufoy 1 901680 02 9   £7.99

SLIDING DOORS
Peter Howitt 1901680 13 4   £7.99

NIL BY MOUTH
Gary Oldman 1901680 03 7   £8.99

NIL BY MOUTH – PHOTO ESSAY
Signed and numbered (hardback)
Gary Oldman 1901680 04 5   £45.00

MY NAME IS JOE
Paul Laverty 1901680 16 9   £7.99

TWENTYFOURSEVEN
Paul Fraser & Shane Meadows 1901680 07 X   £8.99

LOVE AND DEATH ON LONG ISLAND
Richard Kwietniowski 1901680 08 8   £7.99

KEN LOACH FILMOGRAPHY
Ed. James Oliver 1901680 15 0   £6.99

HIDEOUS KINKY
Billy Mackinnon 1901680 29 0   £7.99

WAKING NED DIVINE
Kirk Jones 1901680 29 0   £7.99

American Cinema

THE NINTH CONFIGURATION
William Peter Blatty 1 901680 20 7   £9.99

ONE FINE DAY
Ellen Simon & Terrel Seltzer 1901680 01 0   £7.99

THE BLAIR WITCH : AN ILLUSTRATED HISTORY
Lece Malvey 1901680 44 4   £5.99

OUT OF SIGHT
Scott Frank 1901680 23 1   £8.99

SLAM
Ed. Marc Levin 1901680 27 4   £12.99